DEREK PRINCE

Finding GOD'S WILL

WHITAKER HOUSE

Unless otherwise indicated, all Scripture quotations are taken from the *Holy Bible, New International Version*® NIV®, © 1973, 1978, 1984 by the International Bible Society. Used by permission of Zondervan. All rights reserved. Scripture quotations marked (NASB) are taken from the *New American Standard Bible*®, NASB®, © 1960, 1962, 1963, 1968, 1971, 1972, 1973, 1975, 1977, 1988, 1995 by The Lockman Foundation. Used by permission. (www.Lockman.org). Scripture quotations marked (NASB88) are from the *New American Standard Bible*®, NASB®, © 1960, 1962, 1963, 1968, 1971, 1972, 1973, 1975, 1977, 1988 by The Lockman Foundation. Used by permission. (www.Lockman.org). Scripture quotations marked (NKJV) are taken from the *New King James Version*, © 1979, 1980, 1982, 1984 by Thomas Nelson, Inc. Used by permission. All rights reserved.

Personal pronouns relating to God, Jesus, and the Holy Spirit and some titles of Jesus in Scripture quotations from the *New International Version* have been capitalized to correspond to the overall style used in this book. The forms L͟o͟r͟d and G͟o͟d (in small caps) in Bible quotations represent the Hebrew name for God *Yahweh* (Jehovah), while *Lord* and *God* normally represent the name *Adonai*, in accordance with the Bible version used.

Boldface type in the Scripture quotations indicates the author's emphasis.

F͟ɪɴᴅɪɴɢ G͟ᴏᴅ's W͟ɪʟʟ
(previously titled *God's Will for Your Life*)

Derek Prince Ministries
P.O. Box 19501
Charlotte, North Carolina 28219-9501
www.derekprince.org

ISBN: 978-1-64123-684-3
eBook ISBN: 978-1-64123-695-9
Printed in the United States of America
© 1986, 2021 by Derek Prince Ministries–International

Whitaker House
1030 Hunt Valley Circle
New Kensington, PA 15068
www.whitakerhouse.com

Library of Congress Control Number: 2021935467

No part of this book may be reproduced or transmitted in any form or by any means, electronic or mechanical—including photocopying, recording, or by any information storage and retrieval system—without permission in writing from the publisher. Please direct your inquiries to permissionseditor@whitakerhouse.com.

CONTENTS

1. Jesus, Our Pattern 7
2. A Clear Objective 19
3. Mission Accomplished 31
4. The Culmination: The Cross 43
5. Following Jesus 57

About the Author 71

1

JESUS, OUR PATTERN

The subject of this book is a very personal and practical one: *finding God's will for your life.*

Let me begin by asking you a few questions: Do you have a known, clear objective for your life? Are you just drifting through life, being carried here and there by the winds of habit and fashion? Are you being tossed by waves of circumstances that you can't seem to control?

There is nothing more tragic in a human life than to experience aimlessness. As the saying goes, "If you aim at nothing, you will surely hit it." A person may have talent, intelligence, and special abilities but still accomplish very little of permanent value. Without a clear objective, that individual will experience a life filled with frustration. But it doesn't have to be that way for you and me.

Here is one of the greatest benefits and blessings of the Christian life as God has designed it: He gives each one of us an objective for living. We don't have to feel aimless anymore. God has a purpose for us that is rooted in our faith in Christ.

THE CHRISTIAN LIFE AS A RACE

In the book of Hebrews, we find a wonderful picture of the Christian life:

> *Therefore, since we are surrounded by such a great cloud of witnesses, let us throw off everything that hinders and the sin that so easily entangles, and let us run with perseverance the race marked out for us. Let us fix our eyes on Jesus, the Author and Perfecter of our faith, who for the joy set before Him endured the cross, scorning its shame, and sat down at the right hand of the throne of God.* (Hebrews 12:1–2)

Run Your Race with Endurance

Three important truths are mentioned in these verses. First, the Christian life is a race marked out for us in advance. We do not need to mark out the course; that has already been done for us. We only need to run the race. It is important for us to realize, however, that this race is not a dash or a sprint. It is more like a long-distance marathon.

To be able to run this long race, we must throw off everything that hinders us or gets in our way. These encumbrances may not always be sinful ones. Even so, they can keep us from running our race. We must not only deal with what is sinful in our lives, but we must also eliminate any other weights that would hinder us from fulfilling our service for Jesus Christ. A dedicated runner is physically lean and strips down to the bare minimum—not carrying one ounce of unnecessary weight. Spiritually, we must do the same.

The writer of Hebrews emphasizes that, in order to finish the race, we need a particular quality: *perseverance* or *endurance* (see Hebrews 12:2 NASB, NKJV). Unfortunately, it takes trials and testings to produce endurance in us. But this quality is essential for our survival and success as we walk with the Lord.

We must not only deal with what is sinful in our lives, but we must also eliminate any other weights that would hinder us from fulfilling our service for Jesus Christ.

Fix Your Gaze on Jesus

The second important truth in this passage from Hebrews 12 is that we are to fix our eyes on Jesus as our pattern and inspiration. This truth is stated very clearly in verse 2:

> *Let us fix our eyes on Jesus, the Author and Perfecter of our faith, who for the joy set before Him endured the cross.*

In other words, we can't run the race by self-reliance. We have to look to Jesus. We must put our confidence in Him. He is the only one who will bring us through to victory. If we take our eyes off Jesus for any length of time, we will lose our ability to run the race successfully.

Trust Jesus to Perfect Your Race

Third, we must trust Jesus to perfect our race. Jesus is *"the Author and Perfecter of our faith"* (Hebrews 12:2). He is the one who set it all in motion. We may recognize Jesus as the Author of our faith, but we often lose sight of the fact that He is also the Perfecter of our faith. Jesus not only started everything, but He is also going to work in us to complete the process.

Through my study of Scripture and by the Lord's dealings in my life, I have seen that God never starts anything He is not capable of finishing. We need to take heart and be encouraged by this fact. Jesus started us off on this race, and He is going to enable us to finish it. He is the Author and the Perfecter.

Please keep these three important truths in mind: First, the Christian life is a race in which the course is marked out ahead of us—and it is going to take endurance to complete the race. Second, to be successful, we must fix our eyes on Jesus. He is both our pattern and our inspiration. Third, we must trust Jesus as both the Author and Perfecter of our faith. As long as we keep our eyes on Jesus, He will enable us to keep going—bringing us successfully and triumphantly to the race's finish line.

JESUS'S MOTIVATION: DOING GOD'S WILL

In looking to Jesus as both our pattern and our inspiration in this Christian race, we see that the key to His success was His *motivation*. Unless we really understand His motivation and enter into it *with Him*, we may find this race too much for us.

In Hebrews 10:5–10, the writer applies various quotations from Psalm 40 to Jesus Christ:

Therefore, when Christ came into the world, He said: "Sacrifice and offering You did not desire, but a body You prepared for Me; with burnt offerings and sin offerings You were not pleased. Then I said, 'Here I am—it is written about Me in the scroll—I have come to do Your will, O God.'" First He said, "Sacrifices and offerings, burnt offerings and sin offerings You did not desire, nor were You pleased with them" (although the law required them to be made). Then He said, "Here I am, I have come to do Your will." He sets aside the first to establish the second. And by that will, we have been made holy through the sacrifice of the body of Jesus Christ once for all.

Please notice the word *"body"* near the beginning of this passage. The Lord says, *"Sacrifice and offering You did not desire, but a body You prepared for me."* The writer's comment at the end is, *"By that will* [the will of God fulfilled by Jesus Christ], *we have been made holy through the sacrifice of the body of Jesus Christ once for all."* God provided Jesus with a body to sacrifice on our behalf. (We will explore the theme of sacrifice throughout this book.)

At the core of the above passage, we see Jesus's supreme motivation: *"I have come to do Your will."* That statement was quoted twice for emphasis so it would not be missed. Throughout His earthly life, Jesus's paramount purpose and single objective was *to do the will of God*. He was absolutely clear about it, and He never swerved from it.

Jesus stated the same motivation in John 6:38:

For I have come down from heaven, not to do My own will, but the will of Him who sent Me. (NKJV, NASB)

Jesus specifically came to do the will of God, which was revealed in His eternal purposes. By doing the Father's will, Jesus revealed the Father. This was the way He made known the invisible Father to the world—by doing His will and fulfilling His task.

FULFILLING HIS DIVINE PART

In connection with Jesus doing God's will, a part was written for Him to play: *"Here I am—it is written about Me in the scroll—I have come to do Your will, O God"* (Hebrews 10:7). Before Jesus came to earth, His part was written in the scroll of God's Word.

*By doing the Father's will,
Jesus revealed the Father.*

The *"scroll"* is the prophetic record of Scripture revealing the will of God in the course of Jesus's life. His work, His destiny—all that He was appointed to do—had been set out for Him, and His purpose was to fulfill what had been written.

Jesus did not write His own part or improvise on the script He was given. He discovered His part through His intimate understanding of the Scriptures, and He fulfilled it to perfection.

MAKING THE SACRIFICE

The Father's will for His Son culminated in the sacrifice of Jesus's own body. God's purpose and plan in giving Him a body was that Jesus would offer His body as the perfect sacrifice on behalf of mankind.

Please note the points we have just reviewed:

- Jesus's supreme motivation was to do God's will.
- A part was already written for Him in the scroll of Scripture.
- God's will for Jesus culminated in the sacrifice of His own body.

Each of these points must have a counterpart in our lives. Every one of those statements that was true about Jesus should be true about us. We need the same motivation Jesus had to do God's will—and to discover what is written for us in the scroll of Scripture. Our response—doing God's will in our lives—will culminate with offering our own bodies as *"living sacrifices"* (Romans 12:1).

To close this chapter, let's offer the following prayer together:

> Heavenly Father, thank You for giving each of us a wonderful purpose that is rooted in our faith in Christ—finding and fulfilling Your will for us. May our supreme motivation in life be the same as Jesus's supreme motivation, which was to do Your will as written in the Scriptures and guided by a close relationship with You. We offer our lives to You to do Your will in all things. In the name of Jesus Christ, amen.

FULFILLING THE WILL OF GOD

Practicing God's Will

1. How did you answer the following question, which was presented at the beginning of this chapter: "Do you have a known, clear objective for your life?" Has your answer changed in any way after reading this chapter? If so, in what way? How can you allow God to guide you in His purposes for you?

2. In what way is the Christian life like a race? What kind of race are you currently running?

Seeing God's Will in His Word

Therefore, since we are surrounded by such a great cloud of witnesses, let us throw off everything that hinders and the sin that so easily entangles, and let us run with perseverance the race marked out for us. Let us fix our eyes on Jesus, the Author and Perfecter of our faith, who for the joy set before Him endured the cross, scorning its shame, and sat down at the right hand of the throne of God. (Hebrews 12:1–2)

2

A CLEAR OBJECTIVE

We have learned that one essential condition for a successful life is to have a clearly defined and steadily pursued objective. A person without such an objective is like a boat drifting on the open sea—carried here and there by the winds of habit and the waves of circumstance, without any control over the ultimate destiny.

As I stated earlier, one of the greatest benefits and blessings of the Christian life is that it provides us with a purpose for living. In this respect, Jesus is both our pattern and our inspiration.

COMMITTED TO GOD

Let us now look at how the commitment to do God's will was worked out practically in the earthly life and ministry of Jesus. We will begin with the well-known incident where Jesus met the woman of Samaria at Jacob's Well, which was in the town of Sychar.

Jesus and His disciples were journeying by foot from Judea to Galilee. They passed into Samaria and came to the place that is still known today as Jacob's Well. Apparently, they had run out of food and were hungry, because the disciples had gone into the local town to buy food. Jesus was tired, and He sat down by the well to rest.

When the woman of Samaria came out to the well, she and Jesus had that wonderful conversation in which He gave her the beautiful promise of living water for everyone who was thirsty. Then, Jesus's disciples came back and found Him sitting there talking with the Samaritan woman. The woman was so excited that she left her waterpot, without collecting water, and went back into the town to tell everyone about this remarkable Person she had met at the well.

This is what followed, as described in John's gospel:

> *Meanwhile His disciples urged him, "Rabbi, eat something." But He said to them, "I have food to eat that you know nothing about." Then His disciples said to each other, "Could someone have brought Him food?" "My food," said Jesus, "is to do the will of Him who sent Me and to finish His work. Do you not say, 'Four months more and then the harvest'? I tell you, open your eyes and look at the fields! They are ripe for harvest. Even now the reaper draws his wages, even now he harvests the crop for eternal life, so that the sower and the reaper may be glad together."* (John 4:31–36)

THREE RESULTS OF DOING GOD'S WILL

Please notice Jesus's clear, overarching statement in the above passage: *"My food…is to do the will of Him who sent Me"* (John 4:34). The central motivation of His entire earthly life was *always* to do the will of the One who sent Him. In these verses, Jesus expressed two results of this type of motivation that should have their counterpart in our lives. We will shortly look at a third result in another of Jesus's statements.

Receiving Supernatural Restoration

First, Jesus's commitment to do God's will actually worked supernatural, physical restoration in Him. When He came to the well, He was tired and hungry. Jesus sat down, but instead of eating, He flowed in the will of God in His conversation with this needy woman.

In putting God's will above His own physical needs, He received supernatural replenishment. When the disciples arrived with food, Jesus was not particularly interested in it. He told them, in effect, "I have already eaten." His disciples could not understand what kind of food He had received.

Jesus explained, *"My food…is to do the will of Him who sent Me and to finish His work."* Isn't that a remarkable statement? What does food supply mean to us? It is our source of strength and support. But here is what Jesus was saying: "I have another source that is not natural food. It is doing the will of God, My Father. And when I do His will, that supplies Me with strength and vitality."

Food gives us physical strength and sustains us. However, Jesus said, "Here is what sustains Me and keeps Me going: My commitment to do the will of the One who sent Me." The same can be true for us. Doing the will of

Jesus was saying, "I have another source that is not natural food. It is doing the will of God, My Father. And when I do His will, that supplies Me with strength and vitality."

God can restore us. Setting our will to do God's will can give us strength and purpose.

Gaining a Spiritual Perspective

The second result of Jesus's motivation to do the will of His Father was gaining a different viewpoint. He began to speak about how to look at the world, saying, "You look at the world one way; I look at the world another. You say there are four more months until the harvest, but for Me, the harvest field is already ripe. I am already reaping." Jesus was referring to His encounter with the Samaritan woman. He was reaping a harvest in her village at the very moment He was speaking. A few minutes later, the woman came back with all the people from the village, and Jesus taught them.

The disciples looked at the situation from a purely natural point of view, saying, "It is not yet time for harvest." Do you see the difference between the viewpoint of Jesus and the vision of the disciples? They couldn't see the vision Jesus saw. They could only see in the natural—that the harvest was months away.

In contrast, Jesus had a spiritual viewpoint. He saw conditions from another perspective. He looked at the fields and saw them already *"ripe for harvest"* (John 4:35). Because of His vision, He reaped a wonderful harvest there at the well in Sychar. Jesus's commitment to do God's will was what gave Him this spiritual insight.

Having Impartial Judgment

In the next chapter of John's gospel, we find another statement by Jesus that has much to teach us about the results of being committed to doing God's will. The statement occurs in the middle of Jesus's discussion about the healing of a man who had been paralyzed for many years:

> *I can do nothing on My own initiative. As I hear, I judge; and My judgment is just, because I do not seek My own will, but the will of Him who sent Me.*
>
> (John 5:30 NASB)

Please notice Jesus's words: *"My judgment is just."* He was saying, in other words, "My judgment is right." Why? *"Because I do not seek My own will, but the will of Him who sent Me."* Here we find a third result of the commitment to do God's will. I call it "just judgment" or "impartial discernment."

Jesus was never fooled. Nobody ever deceived Him. Jesus discerned the truth in everyone who came to Him.

He saw into their inner motives, and He knew what they were really after. Whether spiritually or physically, Jesus knew how to reach and touch them where they needed to be touched. This discernment on His part came out of His commitment to do God's will.

How can we avoid foolish judgment and wrong appraisals of people and situations? We find the key in John 5:30, where Jesus said, "My judgment is correct; My discernment is accurate. I see things the way they really are." Why? *"Because I do not seek My own will, but the will of Him who sent Me."*

This is a very important principle for you and me as we fulfill God's will for our lives. We can judge justly—our discernment will be correct—when we are not seeking our own wills. When we are seeking the Father's will, we won't be deceived. We will have accurate perception, discernment, and judgment. It is only when we seek our own wills that we go astray.

Jesus's judgment was not clouded by a desire to get His own way. He was in neutral, so to speak, until the Father moved Him. Jesus waited for the Father's revelation of His will, and then He made a just and accurate judgment, meeting the needs of those whom the Father placed in His path.

*Whether spiritually or physically,
Jesus knew how to reach and touch people
where they needed to be touched.*

Would you like to ask for God's help in this area now? You can do so with the following prayer:

Heavenly Father, I ask You to help me to strengthen my commitment to do Your will daily. May this commitment be worked out in practical ways in my life, as it was in the life of Jesus, so that I receive supernatural restoration, gain a spiritual perspective of my life and the world around me, and have impartial judgment in my relationships with You and other people. Enable me to discern the spiritual and physical needs of those whom You are calling me to serve in Your grace and power. In Jesus's name, amen.

FULFILLING THE WILL OF GOD

Practicing God's Will

1. What are three results of doing God's will? How have you seen these results worked out in a practical way in your life? How can you increase these results?

2. Is there anything keeping you from making a commitment to do God's will? If so, what is it? How will you respond today to God's call to surrender fully to Him?

Seeing God's Will in His Word

Jesus said to them, "My food…is to do the will of Him who sent Me and to finish His work." (John 4:34)

I can do nothing on My own initiative. As I hear, I judge; and My judgment is just, because I do not seek My own will, but the will of Him who sent Me.
(John 5:30 NASB)

3

MISSION ACCOMPLISHED

So far, we have looked at the way Jesus's commitment to do God's will was worked out practically in His earthly life and ministry. We have discovered three specific results in His life from following God's will. First, there was supernatural, physical restoration. At Jacob's Well, Jesus was tired and hungry. Yet, when He did the will of God by sharing the truth with the Samaritan woman, He received physical sustenance. He was no longer hungry when His disciples returned with food.

Second, there was a proper view of the situation. Jesus saw the harvest fields with the eyes of the Father, while His disciples still looked with natural eyes. Jesus's commitment to do the will of God gave Him a view that differed from those around Him.

Third, there was just judgment or impartial discernment. Jesus said, *"My judgment is just, because I do not seek My own will, but the will of Him who sent Me"* (John 5:30 NASB). He was never fooled or carried away by wishful thinking, emotions, or reactions. Jesus always moved in the Father's revelation concerning every situation.

FURTHER RESULTS OF DOING GOD'S WILL

Let's continue our study by looking at two additional results of Jesus's commitment to do the will of God.

Becoming a Channel of Life

The next result is found in Jesus's teaching after He fed the five thousand by multiplying five loaves and two fish.

> *Then Jesus declared, "I am the bread of life. He who comes to Me will never go hungry, and he who believes in Me will never be thirsty. But as I told you, you have*

seen Me and still you do not believe. All that the Father gives Me will come to Me, and whoever comes to Me I will never drive away. For I have come down from heaven not to do My will but to do the will of Him who sent Me. [Again, it is significant that there must be a setting aside of our own wills before we can do God's will.] *And this is the will of Him who sent Me, that I shall lose none of all that He has given Me, but raise them up at the last day. For My Father's will is that everyone who looks to the Son and believes in Him shall have eternal life, and I will raise him up at the last day."* (John 6:35–40)

Jesus had set aside His own will. At the end of His discourse, He referred to doing *"My Father's will."* I have never been able to read the statement *"I am the bread of life"* without being moved. *"Everyone who looks to [Me] and believes in [Me] shall have eternal life, and I will raise him up at the last day."* What a beautiful offer from the One who can feed and give life to a hungry, dying world!

But what was the price Jesus had to pay? Here it is: *"Not to do My will but to do the will of Him who sent Me."* As long as we are busy with our own plans, purposes, and objectives, we cannot be channels of divine life. If we want the privilege of being God's bread, broken to feed a hungry world, then

Jesus said, "Everyone who looks to [Me] and believes in [Me] shall have eternal life, and I will raise him up at the last day." What a beautiful offer from the One who can feed and give life to a hungry, dying world!

---

we must make the same renunciation: *"Not…my will but… the will of Him who sent me."* If this principle was true even for Jesus, how much more so is it true for you and me?

This was the apostle Paul's personal testimony in his second letter to the Corinthians:

> *We always carry around in our body the death of Jesus, so that the life of Jesus may also be revealed in our body. For we who are alive are always being given over to death for Jesus' sake, so that His life may be revealed in our mortal body. So then, death is at work in us, but life is at work in you.* (2 Corinthians 4:10–12)

Paul explained, *"So then, death is at work in us, but life is at work in you."* The world desperately needs channels of life. But there is a price to pay. If we want to be channels of life to others, first, death has to work in us. We cannot have it any other way or change the order. Our own wills, egos, ideas, desires, and ambitions can shut off the life of God. As long as we cling to them, His life cannot flow through us.

The pattern is clear: when death is at work in you, then life is at work in others. You are not here to do your own will—you are here to do the will of Him who sent you.

The will of Him who sent you is to feed and give life to a hungry and dying world. If you will renounce your own will and pursue the will of God for your life with single-hearted devotion, then you, too, can be food and life for a hungry, dying world.

Bringing Glory to God

Another wonderful result was produced in the life of Jesus by His commitment to doing the will of the Father. We discover it in Jesus's great High Priestly Prayer to the Father on behalf of His disciples before His crucifixion. This beautiful declaration by Jesus Christ is found in the latter part of John's gospel:

> *I glorified You on the earth, having accomplished the work which You have given Me to do.*
> (John 17:4 NASB)

In the above verse, the *New American Standard Bible* translates a form of the Greek word *teleios* as "*accomplished.*" This word also means "to finish" or "to complete." "*I glorified You on the earth, having* [finished] *the work which You have given Me to do.*" Throughout the Gospels, Jesus's emphasis was not merely on doing the will of God but also on *finishing* that work. In His encounter with the Samaritan

Throughout the Gospels, Jesus's emphasis was not merely on doing the will of God but also on finishing *that work.*

---

woman at Jacob's Well, Jesus had said, *"My food…is to do the will of Him who sent Me **and to finish His work**"* (John 4:34).

Jesus was always looking ahead to the triumphant conclusion of His task. In His prayer in John 17, Jesus said, in essence, "Now I have brought glory to You, O Father, on the earth, because I have come to the end of the work. I have finished it." Returning to our earlier imagery of running a race, we could say that Jesus was finishing His race. He was just about to break the tape. As He did so, He said, "I have brought glory to God."

FINISHING THE TASK

Doing the will of God always brings glory to Him. When you and I thoroughly finish whatever task God calls us to do, we can bring glory to His name. The task God has assigned to you may be simple, humble, and seemingly ordinary. It may simply entail being the best wife and mother, the most godly husband and father, the most efficient secretary, or the best possible businessperson. Whatever that task may be, if you do a thorough job in finishing it, you will bring glory to God.

A person who is self-seeking or gives half-hearted service to a calling never glorifies God. Why? Because people with selfish motives for serving are always wrapped up in themselves. There are Christians, even ministers, who are more concerned about their own glory than they are about God's glory. Their gifts and ministries may attract large followings, but the ultimate end of such self-focused ministry will not be God's glory.

For us to glorify God, we must have a single vision for the task God has assigned us. In addition, we need to have a fixed determination that we will finish the task—no matter what it costs us. There is nothing I desire more than to come to the end of my ministry and life here on earth and be able to say, in my own limited measure, *"I glorified You on the earth, having accomplished the work which You have given Me to do"* (John 17:4 NASB).

Would you like to pray together to express that same desire?

> Heavenly Father, I want to be a surrendered vessel that can bring Your bread and life to a hungry, dying world. I desire to bring You glory by finishing the call You have given me in this life, with all its various aspects. Grant me a clear and single vision to complete all Your purposes for me. Let me, too, be able to say, at the end of my life, *"I glorified You*

on the earth, having accomplished the work which You have given Me to do." In the name of Jesus, my pattern and inspiration, amen.

FULFILLING THE WILL OF GOD

Practicing God's Will

1. In what ways might your ego and selfish desires and ambitions be preventing God's life from flowing through you? What is the answer to these hindrances?

2. What main task has God assigned to you for your life? How can you demonstrate your commitment to finishing it in order to bring glory to Him?

Seeing God's Will in His Word

We always carry around in our body the death of Jesus, so that the life of Jesus may also be revealed in our body. For we who are alive are always being given over to death for Jesus' sake, so that His life may be revealed in our mortal body. So then, death is at work in us, but life is at work in you. (2 Corinthians 4:10–12)

4

THE CULMINATION: THE CROSS

Our focus has been on Jesus as both our pattern and inspiration for living. We saw that the central motivation of His life was to do God's will as revealed in Scripture. Our key verse for the ultimate purpose that governed Jesus's life is Hebrews 10:7:

> *Then [Jesus] said, "Here I am—it is written about Me in the scroll—I have come to do Your will, O God."*

Again, two vital points are evident: first, Jesus's motivation for coming to earth was to do God's will; second, the part He had to play was already written in the scroll. What makes this truth so wonderful is that in the same "scroll" Jesus referenced, a purpose is outlined for you and me. Our task is to find out what is written for our lives *"in the scroll of the book"* (Hebrews 10:7 NASB).

We also looked at five specific results in the earthly life of Jesus that came through His commitment to do the will of God:

1. He received physical restoration in a supernatural way.

2. He had a proper view of the situation He was in, an outlook that was different from that of the people around Him.

3. He rendered just judgment or impartial discernment. (Jesus was never gullible or deceived. He had an accurate, correct view.)

4. He was a channel of life to a dying world.

5. He glorified God on the earth.

As Jesus attained all these results, He set the pattern for us to follow.

JESUS'S SACRIFICE

Let us now explore the culmination of God's will in the life of Jesus. We return to the tenth chapter of Hebrews, where we previously discovered that God's supreme will for His Son was the sacrifice of His body:

> *Therefore, when Christ came into the world, He said: "Sacrifice and offering You did not desire, but a body You prepared for Me; with burnt offerings and sin offerings You were not pleased. Then I said, 'Here I am—it is written about Me in the scroll—I have come to do Your will, O God.'" First He said, "Sacrifices and offerings, burnt offerings and sin offerings You did not desire, nor were You pleased with them" (although the law required them to be made). Then He said, "Here I am, I have come to do Your will." He sets aside the first to establish the second. And by that will, we have been made holy through the sacrifice of the body of Jesus Christ once for all.* (Hebrews 10:5–10)

Jesus came to this world to do the will of His Father. And the Father prepared a body for Him so that He could accomplish that will. The outworking of God's will demanded that Jesus sacrifice the body God had given Him. The culmination or ultimate goal of Jesus's life was to sacrifice His body on behalf of the world.

DETERMINED TO FINISH

As we have understood from our study so far, Jesus continually emphasized not merely doing God's work, but also finishing it thoroughly and completely. The nearer Jesus came to the end of His earthly ministry, the stronger this emphasis became in His life, as we clearly see in this verse from the gospel of Luke:

> *And it came about, when the days were approaching for His ascension* [literally, "His 'taking up,'" which refers to Jesus being taken up through His death on the cross], *that He resolutely set His face to go to Jerusalem.* (Luke 9:51 NASB88)

Please notice this key phrase: *"He resolutely set His face."* Jesus knew what lay ahead of Him. He had already told His disciples, although they refused to believe Him. As the time

God's supreme will for His Son was the sacrifice of His body on our behalf.

---

of the completion of His work on earth approached, *"He resolutely set His face."* He was determined to finish the work God had given Him.

DAILY DIRECTION

The prophet Isaiah foretold the culmination of Jesus's life on earth as follows:

The Sovereign Lord has given Me an instructed tongue [a disciple's tongue—Jesus was the disciple of the Father], *to know the word that sustains the weary. He wakens Me morning by morning, wakens My ear to listen like one being taught.* (Isaiah 50:4)

Jesus was always in the school of discipleship with the Father. As Jesus spent time in prayer at the beginning of each day, He received His directions for that day from His Father.

Continuing in Isaiah, we read:

The Sovereign Lord has opened My ears, and I have not been rebellious; I have not drawn back. I offered My back to those who beat Me, My cheeks to those who pulled out My beard; I did not hide My face from mocking and spitting. (Isaiah 50:5–6)

It is very important to see that Jesus offered His back to those who beat Him. He freely gave it because this was the Father's will and direction. He heard the Father tell Him, "This is what I sent You to do, My Son," and so He did not withhold Himself from it. He gave Himself over to His torturers.

FACE LIKE FLINT

Where did Jesus receive the determination to complete God's will? From the Father who loved Him. We find this truth in the next verse of Isaiah 50:

Because the Sovereign LORD helps Me, I will not be disgraced. Therefore have I set My face like flint, and I know I will not be put to shame. (verse 7)

Luke reported, *"He resolutely set His face"* (Luke 9:51 NASB88). Writing prophetically seven hundred years earlier, Isaiah had said, *"Therefore have I set My face like flint."* Jesus knew what He was going to endure. In fact, it is clearly expressed in the previous verse of Isaiah: *"I offered My back to those who beat Me, My cheeks to those who pulled out My beard; I did not hide My face from mocking and spitting"* (Isaiah 50:6).

To go through all He had to endure, Jesus would need more than human strength. He would need supernatural strength, and He received it through hearing the Father's voice. Therefore, Jesus was able to say, "My face is set like flint; I am not turning back. No matter what lies ahead, I'm going to go through with it—because My purpose is to do the work the Father has assigned to Me. With His help, I will finish it."

NEARING THE END

Now we come to the actual culmination of Jesus's earthly life. John 19 describes all that He endured in His suffering. Then, after Jesus had been on the cross for three hours or more, He was nearing His end:

Jesus, knowing that all things were now accomplished, that the Scripture might be fulfilled, said, "I thirst!" Now a vessel full of sour wine was sitting there; and they filled a sponge with sour wine, put it on hyssop, and put it to His mouth. So when Jesus had received

*To go through all He had to endure,
Jesus would need more than human strength.
He would need supernatural strength,
and He received it through hearing
the Father's voice.*

---

the sour wine, He said, "It is finished!" And bowing His head, He gave up His spirit. (John 19:28–30 NKJV)

We read in Luke 23:46 that Jesus released His own spirit to the Father. When the soldiers came to break Jesus's legs to hasten His death, they found that He had already died. He had already commended His spirit to the Father.

Earlier, Jesus had told His disciples:

Therefore My Father loves Me, because I lay down My life that I may take it again. No one takes it from Me, but I lay it down of Myself. I have power to lay it down, and I have power to take it again. This command I have received from My Father. (John 10:17–18 NKJV)

IT IS FINISHED!

Before Jesus dismissed His spirit, one of His last great utterances was, *"It is finished!"* (John 19:30 NKJV). *What was finished?* He had finished the task of His earthly assignment.

Throughout His life, Jesus had been saying, *"My food… is to do the will of Him who sent Me and to finish His work"* (John 4:34). In His prayer in John 17, in anticipation of this moment of culmination, Jesus had declared, *"I glorified You on the earth, having accomplished the work which You have given Me to do"* (John 17:4 NASB). This declaration was actually fulfilled on the cross as Jesus cried out, *"It is finished!"*

That exclamation was not a cry of defeat. *"It is finished!"* was a cry of triumph! Jesus was saying, "I have finished everything the Father assigned to Me. I have done it completely. I have left nothing out. Through My sacrifice here on the cross, redemption is now available to all!"

In Greek, *"It is finished!"* is just one word: *tetelestai*. It is the perfect tense of a verb that means "to complete something," "to finish something," "to do something perfectly." In searching for a way to communicate this idea in English, I thought of such phrases as these: "It is completely complete." Or, "It is perfectly perfect." Or, "Everything that had to be done—for man's redemption through the sacrifice of My body—has been accomplished."

Jesus would not release His spirit until He could say, *"It is finished!"* And He would not make that declaration until He knew He had done everything required of Him by the Father. The will of the Father was the goal toward which His life was directed. It was the supreme motivation that had caused Him to set His face like flint. Jesus's commitment to the will of God had enabled Him to go through the shame, pain, rejection, and disgrace of the crucifixion.

I have often heard it said that it was not the nails that held Jesus to the cross, but rather His commitment to the Father's will. He would not swerve from that commitment. Jesus's motivation was to do His Father's will—no matter what He endured. It was His purpose in living here on earth.

God had given Jesus a body. Jesus knew from the Scriptures that God's purpose for His body was that He should sacrifice it on the cross on behalf of mankind. Everything Jesus did was directed to the fulfillment of God's will and the completion of His assignment.

Would you like to pray now for God's strength to fulfill His will for you?

> Heavenly Father, Jesus received from You the determination to complete Your will for His life. You bestowed upon Him supernatural strength to endure even the cross. We ask that You would fill us with Your love and strength to do whatever You have called us to do—no matter what. May we continually live to do Your will. In Jesus's name, amen.

It was not the nails that held Jesus to the cross, but rather His commitment to the Father's will.

FULFILLING THE WILL OF GOD

Practicing God's Will

1. Are you actively attending the "school of discipleship" with the heavenly Father, as Jesus did? Commit to spending time in prayer at the beginning of each day so that you, too, may receive love and direction for that day from your Father.

2. In what area of obedience to God do you find it especially difficult "to set your face like flint" to follow through? Remember that Jesus Himself received supernatural strength and help from the Father to complete His assignment: *"Because the Sovereign LORD helps Me, I will not be disgraced. Therefore have I set My face like flint"* (Isaiah 50:7). As you daily worship and pray to God, ask Him to grant you the supernatural strength to obey Him in all things.

Seeing God's Will in His Word

The Sovereign LORD has given Me an instructed tongue, to know the word that sustains the weary. He wakens Me morning by morning, wakens My ear to listen like one being taught. (Isaiah 50:4)

5

FOLLOWING JESUS

Throughout this book, we have been consistently looking to Jesus as both our pattern and our inspiration. We have seen that Jesus's commitment to do God's will was the motivation that brought Him from heaven to earth.

This commitment shaped and directed the entire course of His earthly life and ministry, culminating in the sacrifice of His own body on the cross.

APPLYING THE PATTERN

Let us now consider how we can apply Jesus's example to our own lives. To follow the pattern Jesus gave us, it is necessary for us to take three main steps.

Choose to Do God's Will

The first step is to choose to do God's will. Jesus stated this truth as He taught in the temple:

If anyone chooses to do God's will, he will find out whether My teaching comes from God or whether I speak on My own. (John 7:17)

The Greek word translated here as *"chooses"* is actually a form of the verb *thelo*, which means "to will" or "to determine." Those who choose to do God's will, or will themselves to do the will of the Father, will find out whether Jesus speaks on His own or from the Father.

Many people underestimate the function of the will in their spiritual lives. They end up being directed by impressions, feelings, and promptings. However, what ultimately determines the direction of our lives is the exercise of our wills. That is the decisive factor. We cannot lead a right life if we do not *will* to lead a right life.

Jesus sets before us a challenge, which is also an invitation. Will you set your will to do God's will? Unless you meet this challenge, you will never lead a right life.

Leading a right life does not come about by being inspired, hearing wonderful preaching, or having somebody pray for us. It comes by our reaching a point in our lives where we make a personal decision. *Decision* is the key word. We have to decide, "I am going to do God's will." Jesus told us, *"If anyone chooses to do God's will, [then] he will find out whether My teaching comes from God."*

It is important to understand that we do not first find out if what Jesus teaches is from God and then set our faces to do God's will. We must first *choose to do* God's will—and then we find out. Many people have the order wrong. They pray, "God, show me the whole matter. I want to understand it all first before I decide to do what You tell me." That is not how the Lord works. He does not scratch an itching intellect. If you just want to know out of intellectual curiosity—without the willingness to make a commitment—God will not reveal His will to you. But, if you will yourself to do God's will, then He gives you understanding, insight, and revelation.

Let me put it another way: commitment leads to understanding, not understanding to commitment. You do not first understand God's will and then commit yourself to do it. You commit yourself to do God's will; then, to your committed mind, God begins to unfold His will.

We must take this vital step for ourselves: "My decision is to do God's will." We cannot say "if" or "perhaps." That is not a commitment. Total commitment is the key that unfolds the will of God in our lives.

Sacrifice Your Body

The second step is to sacrifice your body. For Jesus, the culmination of doing God's will resulted in the sacrifice of His body on the cross. It may surprise you to know that this principle of sacrifice is very clearly stated in Scripture. Romans 12:1 says that for us to do God's will, it will likewise require the sacrifice of our bodies. However, there is a difference between our sacrifices and the one Jesus made. The sacrifice of Jesus's body meant its physical death. We are told by the apostle Paul that our sacrifices require living bodies:

> *Therefore, I urge you, brothers, in view of God's mercy, to offer your bodies as living sacrifices, holy and pleasing to God—this is your spiritual act of worship.*
>
> (Romans 12:1)

*If you will yourself to do God's will,
then He gives you understanding,
insight, and revelation.*

In essence, God says to you and me, "In the light of all I have done for you, the response I require from you is to offer your body to Me as a living sacrifice. Place your body on My altar. Make your body available to Me without reservation."

When you offer your body as a living sacrifice to God, you no longer claim ownership of it. You no longer decide where your body will go or what your body will do, eat, or wear. You have given up the right to make those decisions. From that point on, your body belongs to the Lord. You have sacrificed it to Him—as a living body—on His altar.

Whatever is placed on God's altar belongs thereafter to Him. It no longer belongs to the one who gave it. Again, God requires that, just like Jesus, we sacrifice our bodies. The difference, as we observed earlier, is that Jesus sacrificed His body through death. But we are asked to sacrifice our bodies while they are still alive. We are to hand our bodies over to God and give up our rights and our claims to them.

Sacrificing our bodies may sound very frightening. But I want to tell you that it is actually very exciting. We might picture such a commitment causing us to end up in some lonely wasteland, wearing rags and living on bread and water. But that is not what God has in mind.

> *"For I know the plans that I have for you,"* declares the Lord, *"plans for welfare and not for calamity to give you a future and a hope."* (Jeremiah 29:11 NASB)

God has all sorts of plans for you and your body. But He is not going to tell you these plans until your body belongs to Him. Remember, you must first commit it to Him. Then you will be given understanding.

Renew Your Mind

After offering your body as a living sacrifice, the next step is to renew your mind. Paul described this step very clearly in Romans 12:2:

> *Do not conform any longer to the pattern of this world, but be transformed by the renewing of your mind. Then you will be able to test and approve what God's will is—His good, pleasing and perfect will.*

Once you have taken the decisive step of handing your body over to God as a living sacrifice, something happens in your mind. That decision releases a renewal in which you no longer think the way the world thinks. Worldly people are self-centered in their thinking, so that they wonder, "If I do this, how will it affect me? If I say this, will I get a raise?

*The renewed mind centers on God, asking,
"Will this glorify God?
Is this God's purpose in my life?"*

Will I be promoted? Will people like me?" It all centers on "me." But the renewed mind centers on God, asking, "Will this glorify God? Is this God's purpose in my life?"

"With the mind thus renewed," Paul explained to us, "you can find out the will of God." Our minds are intended to be filled with the knowledge of His will. That knowledge is to completely take control of our thinking. Every motive, every intention, is to be controlled by the knowledge of the will of Jesus Christ.

The reality for us is that God will not give His revelation until we have made this commitment. Our commitment leads to the renewal of our minds. With a renewed mind, we can discern the will of God and find the path He has for us in life.

GOD'S PATH FOR YOU

In most cases, God's path for you will be very different from what you might think. The devil will be right there on your shoulder, whispering in your ear that God's way is going to be miserable and hard.

Satan will tell you that you are going to spend the rest of your life washing dishes or living somewhere in a desert. That might be true—but, most probably, it will not be that way. However, you will never know for sure until you make the commitment.

The outworking of this surrender of your body to God will be the same as it was in the life of Jesus. Remember that there were five results of Jesus's determination to do God's will. You can anticipate the same results in your own life when you surrender your will and body to the Lord.

1. **Jesus received supernatural, physical restoration.** He was not limited to His own physical strength—nor will you be if you are committed to the will of God.

2. **Jesus had proper vision.** He saw everything the way God did—and so will you when you are committed to the will of God.

3. **Jesus had just judgment or clear discernment.** He was not fooled, and He was not deceived. He saw people the way they really were. If you are committed to the will of God, He will give you clear discernment.

4. **Jesus became a channel of life to a dying world.** Likewise, you can be a channel of life when you are committed to doing God's will.

5. **Jesus brought glory to God by finishing His assignment.** He said, *"I glorified You [the Father] on the earth, having accomplished the work which You have given Me to do"* (John 17:4 NASB). If, with all your heart, you will commit yourself to finishing God's work, then you will also be able to glorify God on the earth.

OFFERING YOURSELF TO GOD

Just as Jesus found fulfillment in His earthly life only in doing the will of God, the same will be true for us. If you are experiencing frustration, disharmony, or a lack of peace in your life, it might be time to check on your relationship to the will of God. Your sense of incompleteness may indicate a need for a greater commitment to His will for you.

If you will totally surrender your will and your body to God, yielding any further claim of self-control to Him, it will help you to find deep peace and personal satisfaction in your soul. Even more, you will have the confidence that, in committing your life to Him, you will glorify the Lord by what you say and do. You will discover a new sense of purpose and fulfillment as God reveals His will for your life—and as you glorify Him by completing His assignment for you.

You will discover a new sense of purpose and fulfillment as God reveals His will for your life—and as you glorify Him by completing His assignment for you.

Would you like to affirm that desire by praying a brief but important prayer? If so, let's pray right now:

> Dear heavenly Father, I want Your will for my life. I want to follow the example Jesus set for me as the Author and Perfecter of my faith. Help me to listen to Your voice as He did, drawing strength from You, being set free to follow Your direction, laying aside my own plans, and placing my life on Your altar. By the strength You provide, I take this step now. I give my body and my life to You, Lord. I totally commit myself to Your will and purpose for me. Please bring glory to Yourself as I fulfill Your plan for my life. In Jesus's name, amen.

FULFILLING THE WILL OF GOD

Practicing God's Will

1. In what ways will you apply the pattern of commitment to do God's will that Jesus set for us?

2. How would you now answer the question posed at the beginning of this book: "Do you have a known, clear objective for your life?"

Seeing God's Will in His Word

If anyone chooses to do God's will, he will find out whether My teaching comes from God or whether I speak on My own. (John 7:17)

Therefore, I urge you, brothers, in view of God's mercy, to offer your bodies as living sacrifices, holy and pleasing to God—this is your spiritual act of worship. Do not conform any longer to the pattern of this world, but be transformed by the renewing of your mind. Then you will be able to test and approve what God's will is—His good, pleasing and perfect will. (Romans 12:1–2)

ABOUT THE AUTHOR

Derek Prince (1915–2003) was born in India of British parents. He was educated as a scholar of Greek and Latin at Eton College and King's College, Cambridge, in England. Upon graduation, he held a fellowship (equivalent to a professorship) in Ancient and Modern Philosophy at King's College. Prince also studied Hebrew, Aramaic, and modern languages at Cambridge and the Hebrew University in Jerusalem. As a student, he was a philosopher and a self-proclaimed agnostic.

While serving in the Royal Army Medical Corps (RAMC) during World War II, Prince began to study the Bible as a philosophical work. Converted through a powerful encounter with Jesus Christ, he was baptized in the Holy Spirit a few days later. Out of this encounter, he formed two conclusions: first, that Jesus Christ is alive; second, that the Bible is a true, relevant, up-to-date book. These conclusions altered the whole course of his life, which he then devoted to studying and teaching the Bible as the Word of God.

Discharged from the army in Jerusalem in 1945, he married Lydia Christensen, founder of a children's home there. Upon their marriage, he immediately became father to Lydia's eight adopted daughters—six Jewish, one Palestinian Arab, and one English. Together, the family saw the rebirth of the state of Israel in 1948. In the late 1950s, they adopted another daughter while Prince was serving as principal of a teachers' training college in Kenya.

In 1963, the Princes immigrated to the United States and pastored a church in Seattle. In 1973, Prince became one of the founders of Intercessors for America. His book *Shaping History Through Prayer and Fasting* has awakened Christians around the world to their responsibility to pray for their governments. Many consider underground translations of the book as instrumental in the fall of communist regimes in the USSR, East Germany, and Czechoslovakia.

Lydia Prince died in 1975, and Prince married Ruth Baker (a single mother to three adopted children) in 1978. He met his second wife, like his first wife, while she was serving the Lord in Jerusalem. Ruth died in December 1998 in Jerusalem, where they had lived since 1981.

Until a few years before his own death in 2003 at the age of eighty-eight, Prince persisted in the ministry God had called him to as he traveled the world, imparting God's revealed truth, praying for the sick and afflicted, and sharing his prophetic insights into world events in the light of Scripture. Internationally recognized as a Bible scholar and spiritual patriarch, Derek Prince established a teaching ministry that spanned six continents and more than sixty years. He is the author of more than eighty books, six hundred audio teachings, and one hundred video teachings, many of which have been translated and published in more than one hundred languages. He pioneered teaching on such groundbreaking themes as generational curses, the biblical significance of Israel, and demonology.

Prince's radio program, which began in 1979, has been translated into more than a dozen languages and continues to touch lives. Derek Prince's main gift of explaining the Bible and its teachings in a clear and simple way has helped build a foundation of faith in millions of lives. His nondenominational, nonsectarian approach has made his teaching equally relevant and helpful to people from all racial and religious backgrounds, and his messages are estimated to have reached more than half the globe.

In 2002, he said, "It is my desire—and I believe the Lord's desire—that this ministry continue the work, which God began through me over sixty years ago, until Jesus returns."

Derek Prince Ministries continues to reach out to believers in over 140 countries with Derek's teaching, fulfilling the mandate to keep on "until Jesus returns." This is accomplished through the outreaches of more than forty-five Derek Prince offices around the world, including primary work in Australia, Canada, China, France, Germany, the Netherlands, New Zealand, Norway, Russia, South Africa, Switzerland, the United Kingdom, and the United States. For current information about these and other worldwide locations, visit www.derekprince.org.

Welcome to Our House!

We Have a Special Gift for You

It is our privilege and pleasure to share in your love of Christian books. We are committed to bringing you authors and books that feed, challenge, and enrich your faith.

To show our appreciation, we invite you to sign up to receive a specially selected **Reader Appreciation Gift**, with our compliments. Just go to the Web address at the bottom of this page.

God bless you as you seek a deeper walk with Him!

WE HAVE A GIFT FOR YOU. VISIT:

whpub.me/nonfictionthx

WHITAKER
HOUSE